PRINCEWILL LAGANG

Dangote's Gambit: Unraveling the Business Empire of Aliko Dangote

First published by PRINCEWILL LAGANG 2023

Copyright © 2023 by Princewill Lagang

All rights reserved. No part of this publication may be reproduced, stored or transmitted in any form or by any means, electronic, mechanical, photocopying, recording, scanning, or otherwise without written permission from the publisher. It is illegal to copy this book, post it to a website, or distribute it by any other means without permission.

Princewill Lagang asserts the moral right to be identified as the author of this work.

First edition

This book was professionally typeset on Reedsy.
Find out more at reedsy.com

Contents

1. Dangote's Gambit: Unraveling the Business Empire of Aliko...   1
2. The Foundations of Success   4
3. Dangote Cement - Building the Foundation of an Empire   7
4. Diversification and the Birth of a Conglomerate   11
5. A Continent Transformed - Aliko Dangote's Impact on Africa   14
6. Challenges and Controversies - The Price of Success   17
7. The Future of Dangote's Empire - Legacy and Innovation   21
8. The Dangote Legacy - Lessons and Inspirations   24
9. Africa's Future - Beyond Dangote's Gambit   27
10. Aliko Dangote - The Man Behind the Empire   30
11. Conclusion - A Legacy Unfolding   33
12. A Journey Unfinished   36
13. Summary   39

1

Dangote's Gambit: Unraveling the Business Empire of Aliko Dangote

The sun hung low on the horizon, casting long shadows over the bustling city of Lagos. In the heart of Nigeria's economic hub, a tale of ambition, innovation, and unyielding determination was unfolding. The name Aliko Dangote had become synonymous with wealth, power, and the promise of a brighter Africa. The man behind this empire was no ordinary entrepreneur, and the story of his rise to prominence was nothing short of extraordinary.

Aliko Dangote, born on April 10, 1957, in the ancient city of Kano, had humble beginnings. His grandfather, Alhaji Alhassan Dantata, was a renowned trader, but his father, Mohammed Dangote, a businessman himself, instilled in Aliko the values of hard work and perseverance from an early age. It was these values that would eventually propel him to become the richest man in Africa.

Dangote's journey began with a small trading business in Kano, where he sold sugar, rice, and cement. He quickly realized that the key to success lay in diversification. By the time he was in his twenties, he had expanded his business interests to include commodities like flour, salt, and pasta. He wasn't content with merely importing these goods; he dreamt of producing them on Nigerian soil. It was a daring move that would set the stage for his future success.

The first hint of Dangote's gambit came when he founded the Dangote Group in 1977. At that time, Nigeria was heavily dependent on imports for its basic commodities, and Dangote saw an opportunity to change this. His vision was to make Nigeria self-reliant and less susceptible to the fluctuations of global markets. With this ambition in mind, he ventured into cement production, creating the now-famous Dangote Cement.

Dangote's entry into the cement industry marked the beginning of a monumental shift in the Nigerian and African business landscape. His strategy was simple yet audacious: produce high-quality cement at a lower cost than imports. To achieve this, he invested in modern manufacturing facilities, negotiated favorable trade agreements, and built an extensive distribution network. Dangote Cement quickly became a household name, synonymous with quality, affordability, and innovation.

But Dangote's gambit was far from over. His next move was to diversify further, expanding into industries such as sugar, salt, and even telecommunications. With each expansion, he brought the same unwavering commitment to quality and affordability, transforming industries and inspiring other entrepreneurs to follow in his footsteps. His influence reached far beyond Nigeria, and soon, the name Aliko Dangote became a symbol of African success and self-reliance.

As we delve into the intricacies of Aliko Dangote's business empire, we will uncover the strategic decisions, the partnerships, and the challenges he faced on his path to success. This journey will take us through the highs and lows of building a conglomerate in one of the most dynamic and complex business environments in the world. It will reveal how a man with a dream and a relentless work ethic reshaped the African business landscape.

But as we explore the story of Dangote's gambit, we will also delve into the controversies, the criticisms, and the social responsibilities that come with such immense wealth and power. Aliko Dangote is not just a businessman; he is a symbol of Africa's potential and its challenges, and understanding his empire means understanding the future of a continent on the cusp of transformation.

Join us on this journey as we unravel the intricate web of Dangote's empire, from its humble beginnings in Kano to its global influence, and explore the legacy of a man who dared to dream big and turned his vision into a reality. This is the story of Dangote's gambit, a tale of entrepreneurship, innovation, and the pursuit of a better Africa.

2

The Foundations of Success

In the scorching heat of Kano, Nigeria, where the dust and sweat seemed to blend into an inseparable haze, Aliko Dangote's journey was taking shape. Chapter 2 of our exploration of "Dangote's Gambit: Unraveling the Business Empire of Aliko Dangote" delves into the foundations of his success, revealing the principles and strategies that underpinned his ascent to prominence.

The Kano Years: A Training Ground

Dangote's early years were marked by immersion in the family business. His father's modest trading enterprise introduced him to the art of commerce, and the bustling markets of Kano became his school. It was here that he honed his negotiation skills, developed a keen sense for market trends, and learned the intricacies of supply and demand.

While these experiences may have seemed ordinary at the time, they laid the groundwork for the future tycoon. Dangote's education was not confined to formal classrooms but was deeply rooted in the vibrant markets of Kano. His father's stern guidance, instilling the values of honesty and hard work, further shaped his character and determination.

The Dangote Group: Birth of an Empire

The establishment of the Dangote Group in 1977 was a pivotal moment. It marked the transition from a small trading operation to a full-fledged business conglomerate. Dangote's vision was clear: to become a catalyst for Nigeria's economic growth and self-sufficiency.

A key aspect of his strategy was vertical integration. He wanted to control every stage of the supply chain, from production to distribution. This approach was critical in an environment where infrastructure and logistics were often unreliable. By vertically integrating, Dangote ensured the quality and affordability of his products, making them more accessible to the Nigerian population.

The Cement Revolution: A Game-Changer

The entry into the cement industry was perhaps Dangote's boldest move. Nigeria's dependence on imported cement made it susceptible to global market fluctuations. Dangote aimed to change this by producing cement locally, thereby reducing costs and creating jobs. The opening of the Obajana Cement Plant in 2003, one of the largest in the world, was a testament to his ambition.

To secure the necessary resources for cement production, Dangote invested heavily in limestone mining and partnered with foreign companies to access cutting-edge technology. This investment in infrastructure, technology, and human capital allowed him to drive down production costs, making Dangote Cement more affordable than imported alternatives.

The Power of Partnerships

Dangote understood the significance of strategic partnerships. His collaborations with both local and international companies were instrumental in achieving his goals. He partnered with Sinoma, a Chinese engineering company, to build state-of-the-art cement plants. He also worked with the World Bank's International Finance Corporation to develop Nigeria's cement industry.

Additionally, his relationships with government officials and policymakers were crucial in navigating Nigeria's complex regulatory landscape. Dangote was skilled in leveraging his influence to advocate for policies that would benefit his businesses and the nation's economy as a whole.

Challenges and Triumphs

Despite his remarkable success, Dangote faced numerous challenges along the way. These included infrastructure deficits, political instability, and the unpredictable nature of African markets. However, his unwavering commitment to his vision and his ability to adapt to changing circumstances were key to overcoming these hurdles.

As we delve deeper into the foundations of Aliko Dangote's success, we will see how his principles of hard work, integrity, vertical integration, strategic partnerships, and adaptability were not just the building blocks of his empire but also the cornerstones of his enduring legacy. Chapter 2 unravels the journey from Kano's bustling markets to the inception of the Dangote Group, showcasing the early decisions and strategies that set the stage for Africa's most iconic business empire.

3

Dangote Cement - Building the Foundation of an Empire

The sun rose over Nigeria, casting its golden rays on a nation at the cusp of transformation. Chapter 3 of "Dangote's Gambit: Unraveling the Business Empire of Aliko Dangote" delves into the epic tale of Dangote Cement, the cornerstone of Aliko Dangote's business empire. This chapter explores how he transformed an entire industry and laid the foundation for his unrivaled success.

Vision Realized: Local Cement Production

Aliko Dangote's vision of localizing cement production in Nigeria was a groundbreaking move. Prior to his foray into the cement industry, Nigeria was heavily dependent on imported cement. This reliance made the country vulnerable to global market fluctuations, often leading to high prices and shortages. Dangote sought to change this by producing high-quality cement locally, revolutionizing the construction industry.

The Obajana Cement Plant, situated in Nigeria's Kogi State, became the epitome of his vision. Inaugurated in 2003, it was not only the largest cement plant in Africa but one of the biggest in the world. This ambitious project showcased Dangote's determination to bring Nigeria into a new era of self-sufficiency.

Vertical Integration: Controlling the Supply Chain

Dangote's strategy of vertical integration was at the heart of his success in the cement industry. He aimed to control every aspect of the supply chain, from sourcing raw materials to delivering finished products to consumers. By owning limestone mines, transportation infrastructure, and distribution networks, he ensured the quality and affordability of his cement, reducing costs and making it accessible to the Nigerian population.

One of his most significant achievements was securing a large limestone deposit in Obajana, where the vast majority of Nigeria's limestone resources were located. This gave Dangote Cement a competitive edge, allowing it to produce cement at a lower cost than imports.

Technological Advancements and Quality Assurance

Dangote's commitment to innovation and modernization was evident in his investment in cutting-edge technology. He partnered with international companies, such as Sinoma from China, to install state-of-the-art cement production lines. These technologies not only enhanced production efficiency but also ensured the highest quality standards, meeting international specifications.

Quality control was paramount in Dangote's approach. He implemented rigorous testing and quality assurance procedures to guarantee that Dangote Cement met and exceeded industry standards. This commitment to excellence not only earned the trust of consumers but also positioned his cement as the preferred choice for builders and contractors.

Market Dominance and Competition

Dangote Cement's aggressive expansion into new markets across Nigeria solidified its dominance in the industry. The company strategically positioned its plants in regions with high construction demand, thereby reducing transportation costs and time. This allowed Dangote Cement to maintain competitive prices, a crucial factor in its success.

While Dangote Cement grew exponentially, it faced stiff competition from existing cement producers. The industry was highly regulated, and Dangote had to navigate complex government policies and regulations. His ability to build influential relationships with key policymakers was instrumental in overcoming these challenges.

African Ambitions: Expanding Beyond Nigeria

Dangote Cement's ambitions extended far beyond Nigeria's borders. Dangote envisioned becoming a leading cement manufacturer across Africa, with a focus on nations experiencing rapid urbanization and infrastructure development. He expanded operations to countries like Ghana, Cameroon, and Ethiopia, laying the groundwork for an African cement empire.

The success of Dangote Cement not only transformed the industry but also established Aliko Dangote as a symbol of African entrepreneurial excellence. It showcased the potential of African businesses to compete on a global scale and laid the path for his diversification into other industries, making him the continent's most iconic and influential entrepreneur.

As we conclude Chapter 3, we witness the rise of Dangote Cement as a force to be reckoned with, a testament to the transformative power of vision, vertical integration, technological advancement, and the pursuit of excellence. In the next chapters, we will explore how this foundation set the stage for Aliko Dangote's empire to reach new heights and reshape the African business landscape.

4

Diversification and the Birth of a Conglomerate

With Dangote Cement firmly established as a powerhouse in the African business landscape, Aliko Dangote's ambitions expanded further. Chapter 4 of "Dangote's Gambit: Unraveling the Business Empire of Aliko Dangote" delves into his journey of diversification, exploring how he built a conglomerate that extended beyond the realm of cement, reshaping various industries and economies.

Diversification Strategy: The Road to a Conglomerate

Dangote's entrepreneurial spirit knew no bounds. His philosophy of diversification was simple yet profound: do not put all your eggs in one basket. He recognized the importance of spreading risk and seizing opportunities in diverse sectors. Diversification was not merely a strategy; it was a core principle guiding his business decisions.

Agriculture: A Step into Food Security

Agriculture was a natural choice for diversification, given Nigeria's immense agricultural potential. Dangote ventured into rice and sugar production, setting his sights on reducing the country's dependence on imported staples and ensuring food security.

In the realm of rice, Dangote established Dangote Rice, investing in advanced rice mills and irrigation infrastructure. This initiative aimed to boost local rice production, curb imports, and provide affordable, high-quality rice to Nigerians.

In the sugar industry, he founded Dangote Sugar Refinery, furthering his commitment to self-sufficiency. He understood that a robust sugar industry was essential not only for food production but also for the development of various other industries.

Telecommunications: Connecting a Continent

Dangote's diversification journey extended into the telecommunications sector with the launch of Dangote Communications. With the goal of providing affordable and reliable connectivity, he aimed to bridge the digital divide in Nigeria and beyond.

This endeavor represented a foray into a highly competitive and regulated industry. Dangote's strategy was to offer innovative services and ensure the company's financial stability. His influence and network with key government officials played a pivotal role in navigating the complex telecommunications landscape.

Petrochemicals and Refinery: Fueling the Future

One of Dangote's most ambitious diversification projects was the construction of a petroleum refinery and petrochemical complex. Recognizing Nigeria's vulnerability to global oil price fluctuations and its heavy reliance on fuel imports, he embarked on a quest to make Nigeria a self-sufficient and competitive player in the oil industry.

The Dangote Refinery, expected to be one of the largest in the world, aimed to refine crude oil into a range of products, including gasoline, diesel, and petrochemicals. This venture had the potential to transform Nigeria into a net exporter of refined petroleum products, thereby bolstering the nation's economy and reducing its vulnerability to oil price shocks.

Pharmaceuticals and Healthcare: A Commitment to Wellness

Dangote's diversification journey extended into healthcare with the establishment of Dangote Pharmaceuticals. His vision was to provide affordable, high-quality pharmaceutical products to address the healthcare needs of Nigerians and Africans. The project also included investments in healthcare infrastructure and services, aligning with Dangote's commitment to wellness and social responsibility.

Chapter 4 reveals how Aliko Dangote's strategy of diversification expanded his empire into a conglomerate that transcended industry boundaries. His vision was not only about achieving business success but also about transforming the lives of Nigerians and Africans by creating self-sufficiency, driving economic growth, and providing essential services. As we delve deeper into this chapter, we witness how his diversified empire reshaped entire sectors, economies, and the future of a continent on the rise.

5

A Continent Transformed - Aliko Dangote's Impact on Africa

The story of Aliko Dangote's empire is not just one of personal success, but also a tale of how one man's vision and ambition can reshape an entire continent. Chapter 5 of "Dangote's Gambit: Unraveling the Business Empire of Aliko Dangote" explores the profound impact Aliko Dangote has had on Africa's economic landscape, its people, and its future.

Economic Powerhouse: Driving African Growth

Aliko Dangote's empire has become synonymous with economic power in Africa. His diversified conglomerate has created jobs, stimulated local industries, and reduced dependence on imports, ultimately contributing to the economic growth of not only Nigeria but numerous other African nations. Through his ventures, Dangote has not only made himself one of the richest men in the world but also a symbol of African entrepreneurship and innovation.

Infrastructure Development: Building the Foundations of Progress

Dangote's investments in critical infrastructure have been game-changers for African nations. His extensive road and transportation networks have not only facilitated the movement of goods but have also opened up remote regions for development. In addition, his investments in ports, railways, and other logistics infrastructure have significantly improved trade and connectivity, fostering economic growth and regional integration.

Agricultural Transformation: Nourishing the Continent

Dangote's foray into agriculture, particularly rice and sugar production, has aimed to bolster food security and reduce dependence on imports. By modernizing farming techniques and creating jobs in rural areas, his initiatives have contributed to agricultural transformation, which is vital for feeding Africa's burgeoning population.

Youth Empowerment: Fostering Talent and Skills

Recognizing the potential of Africa's young and dynamic workforce, Dangote has invested in education and skills development. Through scholarships, vocational training centers, and partnerships with educational institutions, he has empowered young Africans with the knowledge and skills they need to participate in the modern economy.

Social Responsibility: Giving Back to Communities

Dangote's commitment to social responsibility goes beyond his businesses. His philanthropic efforts in healthcare, education, and poverty alleviation have made a tangible difference in the lives of many Africans. He has donated substantial funds to combat diseases, build schools and hospitals, and support local communities.

Champion of Women: Empowering Half the Population

Aliko Dangote has recognized the untapped potential of women in Africa's workforce. He has championed women's economic empowerment by supporting initiatives that provide them with training and opportunities. Through these efforts, he has not only promoted gender equality but also contributed to the economic growth of African nations.

Regional Expansion: Beyond Nigeria's Borders

Dangote's ambitions extend far beyond Nigeria. His investments and expansion plans in numerous African countries have elevated him to the status of an African business icon. Dangote Cement, in particular, has left an indelible mark on the continent's infrastructure and construction sectors.

The Legacy of Aliko Dangote: A Beacon of African Progress

As we conclude Chapter 5, we find that Aliko Dangote's impact on Africa extends far beyond his business empire. His vision, ambition, and relentless pursuit of self-sufficiency have transformed nations, created opportunities for millions, and inspired a new generation of African entrepreneurs.

Aliko Dangote stands as a testament to the potential of African business and the capacity for positive change. His legacy is not just one of wealth but one of progress, hope, and the belief that Africa can indeed rise and shine on the world stage. In the next chapters, we will explore the challenges, controversies, and the future of this iconic African entrepreneur and his empire.

6

Challenges and Controversies - The Price of Success

The journey of Aliko Dangote and his business empire is not without its share of challenges and controversies. In Chapter 6 of "Dangote's Gambit: Unraveling the Business Empire of Aliko Dangote," we delve into the obstacles and criticisms that have emerged along the path of his remarkable success.

Industry Dominance and Competition

As Dangote Cement expanded, it faced accusations of monopolizing the market. Critics argued that Dangote's domination in the cement industry could stifle competition, potentially leading to higher prices for consumers and fewer opportunities for other cement producers.

Dangote's response to these concerns was a commitment to maintaining fair pricing and ensuring a level playing field for competitors. He emphasized that his primary goal was to meet the nation's demand for cement and promote economic growth.

Government Relations: Navigating the Political Landscape

Dangote's close relationships with Nigerian government officials have often raised eyebrows. While these connections have undoubtedly facilitated his business ventures, they have also sparked allegations of crony capitalism and favoritism. Critics argue that such connections may hinder transparency and equitable competition.

Dangote has defended his interactions with government officials, emphasizing that they are aimed at addressing the infrastructure and regulatory challenges that affect his businesses. He maintains that these relationships are vital for navigating Nigeria's complex business environment.

Regulatory Hurdles and Policy Implications

Navigating Nigeria's regulatory landscape, riddled with bureaucracy and red tape, has presented significant challenges. Dangote's businesses have sometimes been caught in the crossfire of changing government policies, taxation disputes, and trade restrictions.

These regulatory challenges have necessitated astute negotiation and diplomacy. Dangote's ability to advocate for policies that benefit his businesses while contributing to the nation's economic growth has been crucial in resolving such issues.

Infrastructure Deficits and Security Concerns

Dangote's investments in critical infrastructure, such as roads and ports, have been instrumental in facilitating the movement of goods and people. However, his experiences also shed light on the dire state of Africa's infrastructure, which often necessitates substantial private sector investments.

Security concerns, especially in regions where Dangote operates, have posed challenges. Kidnappings and attacks on company personnel and facilities have required robust security measures, further increasing operational costs.

Environmental and Social Responsibility

Critics have accused Dangote's businesses of not doing enough in terms of environmental sustainability and social responsibility. The heavy industries, such as cement and petrochemicals, have raised concerns about their environmental impact, including emissions and land use.

Dangote has responded by committing to responsible environmental practices and engaging in corporate social responsibility initiatives. These include efforts to mitigate environmental impact, support local communities, and contribute to healthcare and education.

Wealth Disparities and Income Inequality

As Aliko Dangote's personal wealth has grown, questions about wealth disparities and income inequality have become increasingly prominent. Nigeria, like many African nations, grapples with significant economic disparities, and some have questioned whether Dangote's success has exacerbated these inequalities.

Dangote has expressed his commitment to addressing this issue by creating jobs, investing in vocational training, and contributing to economic growth through his businesses.

Chapter 6 highlights the challenges and controversies that have arisen along Aliko Dangote's path to success. It emphasizes that his journey, while remarkable, has not been without criticism and obstacles. As we explore these facets, we also discover how Dangote has adapted and responded to these challenges, reaffirming his commitment to his vision of a transformed Africa. In the upcoming chapters, we will uncover the future of this iconic entrepreneur and his ever-evolving empire.

7

The Future of Dangote's Empire - Legacy and Innovation

As we approach the conclusion of "Dangote's Gambit: Unraveling the Business Empire of Aliko Dangote," Chapter 7 explores the future of Aliko Dangote's empire, his legacy, and the ongoing innovation and expansion that continue to shape the African business landscape.

A Legacy in the Making: A Vision for Generations to Come

Aliko Dangote has consistently emphasized that his empire is not solely about accumulating wealth but about making a lasting impact on Africa. His vision extends far beyond his lifetime, focusing on creating a prosperous, self-reliant, and developed continent for future generations.

Dangote's philanthropic initiatives, investments in education and skills development, and commitment to infrastructure and industrialization are all designed to ensure a lasting legacy. His empire is a reflection of the belief that African entrepreneurs can be the driving force behind the continent's transformation.

Continued Diversification: New Ventures on the Horizon

Dangote's empire is far from static. He continues to diversify and invest in new industries, exploring opportunities in sectors such as fertilizer production, oil and gas, and technology. His entry into these areas not only aligns with Africa's development needs but also positions his conglomerate to adapt to an ever-changing global economy.

The Dangote Refinery and Petrochemical Complex, once completed, is poised to be a game-changer for Nigeria's oil and gas sector, providing significant refining capacity and reducing the country's dependence on fuel imports.

Innovation and Sustainability: Staying Ahead of the Curve

Innovation and sustainability are central to the future of Dangote's empire. Investments in cutting-edge technology, research and development, and environmentally responsible practices are at the forefront of his strategy.

Dangote's commitment to green practices, energy efficiency, and responsible resource management reflects his dedication to the long-term sustainability of his businesses and their positive impact on the environment.

Pan-African Expansion: A Continent-Wide Reach

Aliko Dangote's empire is not limited to Nigeria. He has expanded his businesses across Africa, solidifying his role as a pan-African entrepreneur. His vision extends to becoming a prominent player in multiple African countries, promoting regional economic integration and prosperity.

Dangote Cement, in particular, has left a significant footprint on the African continent, with operations in multiple countries. His commitment to regional expansion is a testament to his ambition to drive economic growth and development across the continent.

THE FUTURE OF DANGOTE'S EMPIRE - LEGACY AND INNOVATION

Global Engagement: Dangote on the World Stage

As the founder of one of Africa's largest conglomerates, Dangote's influence is not confined to the continent. His participation in global forums, collaborations with international organizations, and engagement with foreign governments reflect his ambition to position his empire on the world stage.

Dangote's ventures into the global sugar market and his engagement with foreign investors demonstrate his intention to compete globally and showcase Africa's potential.

Challenges and Adaptation: Navigating the Evolving Business Landscape

The future is not without its challenges. As the global business landscape evolves, Dangote's empire must adapt to changes in markets, technology, and geopolitics. Navigating these shifts will require flexibility, resilience, and strategic thinking.

Dangote's commitment to innovation, diversification, and his ability to harness his influence in various industries and markets will be instrumental in tackling future challenges.

Chapter 7 underscores that the future of Aliko Dangote's empire is one of continual innovation, adaptation, and a steadfast commitment to the transformation of Africa. His journey, marked by challenges and triumphs, is far from over, and his legacy as a visionary entrepreneur and philanthropist is poised to continue shaping the African business landscape and beyond.

8

The Dangote Legacy - Lessons and Inspirations

As we near the end of "Dangote's Gambit: Unraveling the Business Empire of Aliko Dangote," Chapter 8 delves into the enduring legacy of Aliko Dangote, the lessons we can draw from his life and empire, and the inspiration he offers to aspiring entrepreneurs, business leaders, and those passionate about Africa's progress.

Entrepreneurial Resilience: The Power of Perseverance

One of the most profound lessons from Aliko Dangote's journey is the importance of resilience. His path to success was marked by obstacles, challenges, and criticisms, but his determination to overcome these hurdles is a testament to the power of perseverance. Dangote's story illustrates that true entrepreneurs do not let setbacks deter them but use them as stepping stones to success.

Vision and Ambition: Dreaming Big for Africa

Dangote's ambitious vision for transforming not only his own fortune but also the economic landscape of Africa serves as an inspiration. He dared to dream big, not just for himself but for the entire continent. His empire is a testament to the idea that grand visions can be translated into reality with determination and hard work.

Innovation and Adaptation: Staying Ahead in Business

Dangote's commitment to innovation and adaptation is a valuable lesson for the business world. He recognized that staying competitive requires embracing technological advancements, adopting sustainable practices, and remaining open to change. His empire's continued diversification and investment in new sectors showcase the importance of evolving with the times.

Social Responsibility and Philanthropy: Giving Back to Society

The philanthropic initiatives of Aliko Dangote underline the responsibility that comes with success. He has not only built a business empire but also used his wealth to make a positive impact on communities, healthcare, education, and more. Dangote's legacy serves as a reminder that those who have the means to give back to society have a duty to do so.

African Leadership and Global Engagement: Africa's Voice on the World Stage

Dangote's engagement on the global stage showcases the potential of African leaders and entrepreneurs to play a significant role in international affairs. His ability to navigate the complex web of geopolitics and foreign investments positions him as an influential voice for Africa's progress.

Continuity and Legacy Building: Passing the Baton

Aliko Dangote's legacy is not solely about his own achievements but also about creating a lasting impact for future generations. His commitment to education, skills development, and infrastructure sets the stage for a brighter Africa. It also highlights the importance of building a legacy that endures beyond one's lifetime.

Inspiration for Future Entrepreneurs: A Role Model for Africa's Youth

Perhaps the most significant contribution of Aliko Dangote's journey is the inspiration he offers to Africa's youth. As an icon of African entrepreneurship and success, he demonstrates that with vision, hard work, and dedication, young Africans can build their dreams and drive the continent's progress.

Chapter 8 serves as a reflection on the enduring legacy of Aliko Dangote, his contributions to Africa and the global business landscape, and the inspiration he provides for individuals with dreams of making a positive impact on the world. His story reminds us that the journey of a single entrepreneur can indeed reshape a continent's destiny.

9

Africa's Future - Beyond Dangote's Gambit

As we conclude our exploration of "Dangote's Gambit: Unraveling the Business Empire of Aliko Dangote," Chapter 9 looks forward to Africa's future, beyond the remarkable story of one man and his empire. It reflects on the broader implications of Dangote's journey for the continent and the potential for continued growth, innovation, and transformation.

Economic Independence and Self-Sufficiency: A Continent's Aspiration

Aliko Dangote's empire is emblematic of Africa's quest for economic independence and self-sufficiency. His achievements show that the continent possesses the talent, resources, and entrepreneurial spirit required to foster development and reduce reliance on imports.

African Entrepreneurship: A Rising Force in the Global Economy

Dangote's journey highlights the growing influence of African entrepreneurs on the global stage. His success demonstrates that Africa can produce leaders who not only transform their nations but also play pivotal roles in international commerce and diplomacy.

Regional Integration and Collaboration: Africa's Key to Progress

Dangote's expansion into multiple African countries underscores the importance of regional integration. As African entrepreneurs like Dangote collaborate with neighboring nations, they can drive economic growth, harmonize policies, and create a more connected and prosperous continent.

Youth Empowerment and Skills Development: The Next Generation's Promise

The investments Aliko Dangote has made in education and skills development represent a foundation for Africa's future. Empowering the next generation of leaders through education, training, and opportunities will be crucial for the continent's continued growth.

Innovation and Sustainability: Building a Resilient Africa

The commitment to innovation and sustainability displayed by Dangote's empire offers a blueprint for a more resilient Africa. Embracing technological advancements and responsible practices can help the continent adapt to change, mitigate environmental impact, and reduce dependence on volatile global markets.

Social Responsibility and Philanthropy: Building a Caring Continent

Aliko Dangote's dedication to social responsibility and philanthropy sets an example for other African business leaders. The culture of giving back to society can help address pressing challenges and inequalities while fostering a more compassionate and equitable Africa.

The Ongoing Dangote Legacy: A Continuation of Transformation

The legacy of Aliko Dangote is not a closed chapter but an ongoing narrative. As he continues to diversify and innovate, his empire will remain a driving force in shaping Africa's destiny, offering hope and inspiration for those who dream of a brighter future for the continent.

Chapter 9 marks the conclusion of "Dangote's Gambit" and offers a reflection on the broader implications of Aliko Dangote's journey. His empire's remarkable story serves as a symbol of Africa's potential and resilience, and it represents the ever-evolving narrative of a continent poised for greatness.

10

Aliko Dangote - The Man Behind the Empire

As we reach the final chapter of "Dangote's Gambit: Unraveling the Business Empire of Aliko Dangote," we take a closer look at the man himself, the vision, principles, and personal attributes that have driven his success, and the enduring impact he leaves on Africa and the world.

Visionary Leadership: A Vision Bigger Than Himself

Aliko Dangote's journey is characterized by visionary leadership. His vision extends far beyond personal wealth; it is about creating a better Africa. He has demonstrated that leaders with a clear, ambitious vision can inspire others and drive significant change.

Relentless Determination: A Force for Progress

Dangote's story is a testament to the power of determination. His ability to overcome challenges, setbacks, and obstacles reflects the unwavering commitment to his goals. He serves as a role model for those who understand that determination is often the key to success.

Innovation and Adaptation: The Keys to Staying Relevant

Aliko Dangote's empire is marked by its commitment to innovation and adaptation. He recognizes that staying competitive in an evolving world requires embracing change and being open to new ideas and technologies.

Social Responsibility and Philanthropy: A Heart for Others

Dangote's philanthropic efforts demonstrate a deep sense of social responsibility. He has used his wealth to make a positive impact on communities, showing that success is not just about financial gain but about helping those in need.

African Identity and Patriotism: A Champion for the Continent

Dangote's journey has been marked by a deep sense of African identity and patriotism. He is a champion for the continent, striving to promote self-reliance and reduce Africa's dependence on imports. His story is a testament to the potential of Africans to transform their own destiny.

Global Engagement and Diplomacy: An Ambassador for Africa

Aliko Dangote's engagement on the global stage makes him an ambassador for Africa. He has shown how African leaders and entrepreneurs can navigate the complexities of international relations and foreign investments to promote the continent's growth.

The Dangote Legacy: A Beacon of Inspiration

Aliko Dangote leaves behind a legacy of inspiration. His journey is not just a story of personal success but a testament to the potential of African entrepreneurship. He inspires individuals to dream big, work hard, and contribute to Africa's progress.

The Future Beyond Dangote: Africa's Ongoing Transformation

Aliko Dangote's journey is not the end but a chapter in Africa's ongoing transformation. His success paves the way for future entrepreneurs, leaders, and individuals who aspire to make a difference on the continent.

In this final chapter, we celebrate Aliko Dangote as a visionary leader, a symbol of African entrepreneurship, and a man who has made a profound impact on the continent and the world. His story serves as an enduring source of inspiration for those who dream of a brighter future for Africa.

11

Conclusion - A Legacy Unfolding

As we conclude our journey through "Dangote's Gambit: Unraveling the Business Empire of Aliko Dangote," Chapter 11 offers a reflection on the enduring legacy of Aliko Dangote and the continuing impact of his empire on Africa and the world. It is a testament to the idea that the story of Aliko Dangote is far from over, but rather a legacy that continues to unfold.

The Ongoing Dangote Empire: A Story of Evolution

Aliko Dangote's empire is dynamic, constantly evolving, and diversifying. His businesses continue to expand into new sectors, embracing innovation and sustainability. The empire reflects the ever-changing landscape of African entrepreneurship.

A Symbol of African Excellence: Inspiring the Next Generation

Dangote's journey stands as a symbol of African excellence and a beacon of inspiration for the next generation of African entrepreneurs. His success demonstrates that Africa can produce leaders who not only transform their nations but also play pivotal roles in the global business arena.

African Economic Transformation: Self-Reliance and Prosperity

Aliko Dangote's emphasis on economic self-reliance and prosperity resonates with Africa's aspirations. His journey exemplifies that with determination, vision, and innovation, Africa can reduce dependence on imports, stimulate economic growth, and create opportunities for its people.

Global Engagement and Diplomacy: Africa's Voice on the World Stage

Dangote's role as a global business leader showcases the influence and potential of African entrepreneurs and leaders on the world stage. His engagements in foreign investments, partnerships, and global forums amplify Africa's voice in international affairs.

The Power of Philanthropy: Making a Positive Impact

Aliko Dangote's philanthropic efforts underscore the importance of giving back to society. They are a reminder that those with the means to make a difference have a responsibility to do so, particularly in addressing critical challenges and inequalities.

A Continuation of Transformation: Beyond the Empire

Aliko Dangote's journey is not just a story of wealth and business success but a narrative of transformation and a lasting legacy. The empire he has built serves as a foundation for Africa's future, ensuring that his vision of a prosperous, self-reliant continent endures.

Africa's Ascent: A Bright Future Beckons

As we conclude "Dangote's Gambit," we find that the story of Aliko Dangote is not just about one man's empire but about Africa's ascent on the global stage. The future beckons with hope and promise, underpinned by the vision, principles, and determination of African leaders and entrepreneurs like Dangote.

In this final chapter, we celebrate Aliko Dangote as a visionary leader, a symbol of African entrepreneurship, and a man whose legacy continues to shape Africa's destiny. His story is an enduring source of inspiration for those who dream of a brighter future for the continent and the world.

12

A Journey Unfinished

In our final chapter of "Dangote's Gambit: Unraveling the Business Empire of Aliko Dangote," we acknowledge that Aliko Dangote's story is a journey unfinished. His enduring legacy and impact on Africa and the global business landscape continue to evolve, setting the stage for a future that holds promise, challenges, and opportunities.

The Ever-Evolving Empire: A Story of Adaptation

Aliko Dangote's empire is a testament to the importance of adaptation and innovation. As it continues to diversify, embrace new technologies, and respond to changing markets, it embodies the notion that business success hinges on the ability to evolve.

Inspiring the Next Generation: A Legacy of African Entrepreneurship

Dangote's story stands as an enduring source of inspiration for the next generation of African entrepreneurs. His journey demonstrates that Africa has the potential to produce leaders who not only transform their own nations but also shape the trajectory of the entire continent.

The Quest for Economic Transformation: A Vision for Prosperity

Aliko Dangote's emphasis on economic self-reliance and prosperity aligns with the aspirations of Africa. His journey showcases that with determination, vision, and an unwavering commitment to self-sufficiency, the continent can achieve sustainable economic growth.

Africa's Global Role: A Voice on the World Stage

Dangote's presence on the global business scene amplifies the influence and potential of African entrepreneurs and leaders. His engagements in international investments, partnerships, and forums underscore Africa's growing significance in global affairs.

Social Responsibility and Philanthropy: Making a Difference

Dangote's philanthropic efforts emphasize the importance of giving back to society. His contributions to healthcare, education, and community development serve as a reminder that those who have the means to make a difference have a responsibility to do so.

Continuity and Legacy Building: Beyond Aliko Dangote

Aliko Dangote's journey is not just about his personal success but about creating a legacy that endures beyond his lifetime. His commitment to education, skills development, and infrastructure lays the foundation for Africa's future.

Africa's Ascent: A Bright and Complex Future

In this final chapter, we acknowledge that Aliko Dangote's journey is a testament to Africa's ascent on the global stage. The future is both bright and complex, filled with challenges and opportunities. Africa's trajectory will be shaped by leaders and entrepreneurs who, like Dangote, dream big, work hard, and strive for a brighter future.

As we conclude "Dangote's Gambit," we recognize that Aliko Dangote's story is one of an unfinished journey. His legacy continues to evolve, and the impact of his empire on Africa and the world will endure. The narrative of African entrepreneurship and transformation is a story that remains in progress, with a bright future beckoning.

13

Summary

"Dangote's Gambit: Unraveling the Business Empire of Aliko Dangote" is an exploration of the life, career, and impact of Aliko Dangote, one of Africa's most successful and influential entrepreneurs. The book consists of twelve chapters that delve into various aspects of his journey and legacy.

Throughout the book, we follow Aliko Dangote's rise from a modest family background to becoming one of the wealthiest individuals in the world. His journey is marked by visionary leadership, relentless determination, and a commitment to transforming Africa's economic landscape.

Key themes and highlights from each chapter include:

1. Chapter 1: A Vision Takes Root
   - Introduction to Aliko Dangote and his early life.
   - The emergence of Dangote Cement and its significance.

2. Chapter 2: The Cement King
   - Dangote's ascendancy in the cement industry.
   - His vision for self-sufficiency in cement production in Nigeria.

3. Chapter 3: The Path to Success
   - An exploration of Dangote's entrepreneurial journey.
   - The challenges and triumphs he faced on his way to success.

4. Chapter 4: Diversification and the Birth of a Conglomerate
   - Dangote's strategy of diversification into agriculture, telecommunications, petrochemicals, and pharmaceuticals.
   - The impact of his diversified empire on various sectors.

5. Chapter 5: A Continent Transformed - Aliko Dangote's Impact on Africa
   - Dangote's role in driving economic growth, infrastructure development, and agricultural transformation across Africa.
   - His commitment to youth empowerment, women's economic empowerment, and social responsibility.

6. Chapter 6: Challenges and Controversies - The Price of Success
   - An examination of the challenges and criticisms Dangote faced, including accusations of monopolization and government relations.
   - How he navigated regulatory hurdles and addressed environmental and social responsibility concerns.

7. Chapter 7: The Future of Dangote's Empire - Legacy and Innovation
   - Dangote's ongoing diversification, innovation, and commitment to sustainability.
   - His expansion across Africa and engagement on the global stage.

8. Chapter 8: The Dangote Legacy - Lessons and Inspirations
   - Lessons from Dangote's journey, including resilience, innovation, and social responsibility.
   - His role as an inspiration for the next generation of African entrepreneurs.

9. Chapter 9: Africa's Future - Beyond Dangote's Gambit
   - The broader implications of Dangote's journey for Africa's economic

independence, entrepreneurship, and regional integration.

- The importance of empowering youth, fostering innovation, and embracing social responsibility.

10. Chapter 10: Aliko Dangote - The Man Behind the Empire

- A closer look at Dangote's visionary leadership, determination, and commitment to innovation and sustainability.

- His role as an ambassador for Africa on the global stage and his enduring impact.

11. Chapter 11: Conclusion - A Legacy Unfolding

- A reflection on the evolving empire of Aliko Dangote and its impact on Africa and the world.

- The inspiration he offers to future generations and the promise and challenges that lie ahead for the continent.

12. Chapter 12: A Journey Unfinished

- A recognition that Dangote's story is a journey still in progress, characterized by adaptation, inspiration, and a commitment to Africa's economic transformation.

- The bright and complex future that awaits Africa, with its trajectory shaped by visionary leaders and entrepreneurs like Aliko Dangote.

In summary, "Dangote's Gambit" is a comprehensive exploration of Aliko Dangote's life, empire, and the enduring legacy he leaves on Africa and the world. It emphasizes the potential of African entrepreneurship, self-sufficiency, and global influence, offering lessons and inspiration for those who aspire to make a positive impact on the continent's future.

www.ingramcontent.com/pod-product-compliance
Lightning Source LLC
LaVergne TN
LVHW012132070526
838202LV00056B/5960